On Family Wealth

ON FAMILY WEALTH

Lewis Worrow

Contents

Foreword

In the annals of human history, the study of wealth—its creation, preservation, and transmission—has often been overshadowed by the more immediate concerns of survival and societal development. Philosophers, economists, and historians have periodically touched upon the subject, yet a comprehensive exploration of family wealth, particularly through the lens of evolutionary psychology, remains relatively rare.

The quest for understanding family wealth involves delving into the deepest recesses of human nature and societal evolution. From the strategic marriages of the aristocracy to the modern practices of wealth management, the principles guiding these actions are rooted in our biology and psychology. The desire to secure resources, elevate social status, and ensure the well-being of our progeny is an innate drive that has been shaped by millennia of evolution.

In classical thought, wealth was often viewed with suspicion or ambivalence. Plato, in his dialogues, emphasised the pursuit of higher ideals over material gain (see: Republic, Symposium). Aristotle, while acknowledging the role of wealth in achieving the good life, warned against its excesses and the moral decay it could bring (Nicomachean Ethics, Book IV). Medieval and Renaissance thinkers such as Augustine and Aquinas integrated these classical perspectives into a Christian framework, where wealth was seen as both a divine blessing and a potential source of sin.

Modern thinkers began to scrutinise the mechanisms and morality of wealth more rigorously. Adam Smith's pioneering work in economics laid the foundation for understanding the dynamics of markets and the creation of wealth (The Wealth of Nations). Later, Marxist critiques highlighted the disparities and conflicts arising from wealth accumulation (Das Kapital). Contemporary scholars like Thomas Piketty have further examined the historical trends and future trajectories of wealth inequality (Capital in the Twenty-First Century).

However, it is only through the lens of evolutionary psychology that we can fully appreciate the profound and often subconscious forces driving our economic behaviours. Influenced by the works of David Buss and other evolutionary psychologists, this book seeks to uncover the deep-seated motivations that have guided human beings in their quest for wealth across generations.

On Family Wealth explores these themes with scholarly rigour and philosophical depth. It bridges the empirical research from psychology and economics with reflective insights into human nature, offering a comprehensive framework for understanding the intricate dynamics of family wealth.

In this book, you will find a synthesis of knowledge that spans multiple disciplines, providing a rich tapestry of insights into how wealth is created, preserved, and transmitted within families. The principles discussed herein are not merely theoretical but are grounded in empirical research and historical examples, ensuring their practical applicability.

As you engage with the chapters that follow, you will encounter a profound exploration of the human condition, the evolutionary imperatives that shape our behaviours, and the strategic considerations essential for building and sustaining family wealth. This journey through the intellectual landscape of wealth will equip you with the knowledge and insights needed to navigate the complexities of economic life.

On Family Wealth is more than a guide; it is a philosophical inquiry into one of the most fundamental aspects of human existence. I invite you to embark on this journey with an open mind, ready to explore the depths of human nature and the intricate mechanisms of wealth that have shaped our history and will continue to influence our future.

In this exploration, you will also discover the pivotal role of cultural norms and societal structures in shaping wealth dynamics. Different cultures have varying approaches to inheritance, philanthropy, and wealth distribution, all of which reflect their unique histories and values. Understanding these cultural contexts not only provides a richer perspective on how wealth functions within societies but also highlights the adaptability and resilience of human economic behaviour. This book delves into comparative analyses, drawing on examples from across the globe to illustrate the diverse strategies employed by families to maintain and grow their wealth through generations.

Moreover, On Family Wealth addresses the future of wealth in the context of rapid technological advancements and globalisation. The digital revolution has introduced new opportunities and challenges in wealth management, from cryptocurrency and blockchain to artificial intelligence and automation. These innovations are reshaping traditional notions of wealth, offering novel avenues for accumulation and preservation, while also posing significant risks. By examining these emerging trends, this book provides a forward-looking perspective, equipping readers with the insights necessary to navigate an increasingly complex and interconnected economic landscape. As we stand on the brink of unprecedented change, understanding the evolutionary and psychological underpinnings of wealth becomes ever more crucial for making informed decisions that will shape the future of family wealth for generations to come.

Evolutionary Foundations
of Wealth

1.1 Overview of Evolutionary Psychology

Evolutionary psychology is a theoretical approach that seeks to explain useful mental and psychological traits—such as memory, perception, and language—as adaptations that arose through natural selection. This field, championed by scholars, bridges the gap between biology and psychology by applying principles of evolutionary theory to understand the human mind and behaviour.

According to evolutionary psychology focuses on four key questions:

1. Why is the mind designed the way it is?
2. How is the human mind designed?
3. What are the functions of its component parts?
4. How does input from the current environment interact with the design of the human mind to produce observable behaviour?

These questions guide the exploration of how evolutionary pressures have shaped the psychological mechanisms underlying human behaviour, including our approaches to wealth accumulation and management.

1.2 The Role of Wealth in Human Evolution

Wealth, in the context of human evolution, encompasses more than just financial resources; it includes any assets that enhance an individual's survival and reproductive success. In ancestral environments, wealth could mean access to food, territory, social alliances, or mates. Modern financial wealth is an extension of these primal resources.

Human beings have evolved various psychological mechanisms to accumulate and manage wealth. These mechanisms include risk-taking, cooperation, and competition—traits that have been crucial for survival and reproduction throughout human history. For example, cooperative behaviours can lead to mutually beneficial alliances, while competitive behaviours can help secure resources from rivals.

Evidence and Theoretical Background

The study of wealth from an evolutionary perspective is supported by extensive research in psychology, anthropology, and biology. For instance, studies show that humans tend to prefer traits in mates that signal resource availability and stability, such as physical health and social status. This preference can be traced back to the need for ensuring the well-being of offspring (Buss, 2019).

Additionally, anthropological studies of hunter-gatherer societies reveal that resource-sharing and social alliances were fundamental for survival. Individuals who were able to amass resources and share them within their social group gained social status and support, which increased their reproductive success (Buss, 2019).

1.3 Objectives and Scope of the Book

This book aims to explore the evolutionary psychology behind how humans accumulate and preserve wealth. It examines the primal instincts and psychological mechanisms that drive financial behaviours, tracing the biological and psychological imperatives shaped by natural selection that influence modern wealth-building strategies.

Through the lens of evolutionary theory, the book delves into survival strategies and resource management instincts that manifest in contemporary financial practices. Integrating research from psychology, biology, and economics, it offers a clear understanding of the innate human tendencies guiding economic actions.

1.4 Methodology and Approach

The methodology adopted in this book involves a multidisciplinary approach, combining insights from evolutionary psychology, behavioural economics, and anthropology. By examining both historical data and contemporary case studies, the book provides a comprehensive analysis of how evolutionary principles continue to shape human financial behaviour.

The Origins of Wealth

2.1 Evolutionary Roots of Resource Accumulation

Wealth accumulation is not a modern phenomenon; it has deep evolutionary roots. Throughout human history, individuals and groups have sought to gather and control resources essential for survival and reproduction. These resources include food, territory, mates, and social alliances. The drive to accumulate wealth is deeply embedded in our biology and is a fundamental aspect of human nature.

From an evolutionary perspective, the accumulation of resources provided several advantages. It increased an individual's or group's chances of survival during times of scarcity, enhanced their social status, and made them more attractive to potential mates. These benefits are reflected in the behaviour of our ancestors and continue to shape human actions today.

2.2 Historical Perspectives on Wealth Creation

Historically, wealth creation has taken many forms. In hunter-gatherer societies, wealth was measured by the amount of food and resources one could gather and share within the group. Sharing resources built social bonds and ensured mutual survival, as observed in studies of modern hunter-gatherer groups such as the !Kung and the Hadza. With the advent of agriculture, wealth became tied to land ownership and the ability to produce surplus food. This shift allowed for the accumulation of goods, leading to the development of trade and the rise of complex societies.

The control of land and resources became synonymous with power and social status, setting the stage for the economic systems we see today.

2.3 The Role of Natural Selection in Wealth Dynamics

Natural selection has played a crucial role in shaping the behaviours associated with wealth accumulation. Individuals who were more effective at gathering and protecting resources were more likely to survive and pass on their genes. This selective pressure led to the development of psychological traits that favour resource acquisition and management.

Evidence from Evolutionary Psychology

Evolutionary psychologists have provided extensive evidence on how natural selection influences economic behaviours. For example, traits such as risk-taking, strategic thinking, and social intelligence are advantageous for resource acquisition. These traits have been favoured by natural selection and are prevalent in individuals who are successful in accumulating wealth (Buss, 2019).

2.4 Mechanisms of Wealth Accumulation

Several psychological mechanisms underpin the human drive to accumulate wealth:

1. **Risk-Taking**: Evolutionarily, taking risks could lead to high rewards. Individuals who were willing to take calculated risks often gained more resources, though this also came with the potential for significant losses. Modern financial markets reflect this dynamic, where investors take risks to achieve high returns.
2. **Social Alliances**: Forming alliances and networks has always been crucial for resource acquisition and protection. In ancestral environments, alliances provided safety and support, which increased chances of survival. Today, social networks and professional relationships continue to play a vital role in wealth creation.
3. **Reciprocity and Trust**: Trust and reciprocal relationships are foundational for cooperative behaviour. Humans have evolved to remember and reciprocate acts of kindness, which helps in building long-term alliances. This mechanism is evident in business practices where trust and reputation are critical for success.
4. **Strategic Thinking**: The ability to plan and strategize is a significant advantage in resource acquisition. This includes anticipating future needs, managing resources efficiently, and navigating social dynamics. Strategic thinking is a hallmark of successful individuals and organisations.

2.5 Case Studies on Wealth Dynamics

To illustrate the principles of evolutionary psychology in wealth accumulation, we can examine historical and contemporary case studies:

- **Historical Case Study: The Medici Family:** The Medici family of Renaissance Florence accumulated vast wealth and power through strategic marriages, political alliances, and patronage of the arts. Their ability to navigate social and economic landscapes reflects key evolutionary strategies for resource management.
- **Contemporary Case Study: Warren Buffett:** Warren Buffett, one of the world's wealthiest individuals, exemplifies the principles of risk-taking, strategic thinking, and social alliances. His investment strategies and business acumen have allowed him to accumulate and sustain his wealth over decades.

Conclusion

The origins of wealth accumulation are deeply rooted in evolutionary history. Understanding the evolutionary mechanisms that drive resource acquisition provides valuable insights into human economic behaviour. By examining both historical and contemporary examples, we can see how these principles continue to influence wealth creation in modern society.

Reputation and Social Capital

3.1 The Evolutionary Importance of Reputation

Reputation plays a crucial role in human social dynamics. From an evolutionary perspective, reputation serves as a signal of an individual's qualities, such as trustworthiness, competence, and social value. In ancestral environments, a strong reputation could mean the difference between life and death, as it influenced social alliances, mate selection, and resource sharing.

Reputation is built through consistent behaviours that signal one's qualities to others. Evolutionary psychology suggests that humans are naturally attuned to reputational cues because they help navigate social hierarchies and form alliances. A strong reputation can deter adversaries and attract allies, much like the status signals observed in other primates.

3.2 Building and Maintaining Reputation

Building and maintaining a reputation involves several strategies rooted in evolutionary psychology:

1. **Consistency in Behaviour**: Consistent behaviour over time helps build trust and reliability. Studies have shown that individuals who display consistent behaviours are more likely to be trusted and respected by their peers (Tomasello, 2009).
2. **Public Displays of Virtue**: Public acts of generosity, fairness, and bravery can enhance

reputation. These displays signal to others that an individual is a valuable ally. For example, hunter-gatherer societies often celebrate individuals who share their resources, reinforcing the importance of generosity in reputation building (Buss, 2019).

3. **Reciprocity**: Engaging in reciprocal relationships strengthens social bonds and builds reputation. Reciprocity involves returning favours and helping those who have helped you, which fosters long-term cooperative relationships.

4. **Social Intelligence**: The ability to read social cues and navigate complex social dynamics is critical for maintaining a positive reputation. Individuals with high social intelligence can better understand the needs and intentions of others, allowing them to act in ways that enhance their social standing.

3.3 Social Signalling and Status

Social signalling theory explains how individuals use behaviours and traits to signal their qualities to others. These signals help establish and maintain social hierarchies. In the context of wealth and reputation, social signalling can take various forms, including:

1. **Conspicuous Consumption**: Displaying wealth through luxury goods and services signals high social status. This behaviour is rooted in evolutionary psychology, where visible resources

could attract mates and deter rivals (Veblen, 1899).

2. **Altruism**: Acts of altruism can enhance reputation by signalling that an individual is willing to invest resources in the well-being of others. This behaviour is particularly effective in building social capital and fostering cooperative relationships.

3. **Competence and Achievement**: Demonstrating competence in valuable skills or achieving significant milestones can enhance reputation. Individuals who excel in their fields are often respected and admired, leading to increased social status and influence.

3.4 Case Studies on Reputation and Wealth

To illustrate the principles of evolutionary psychology in reputation building, we can examine historical and contemporary case studies:

- **Historical Case Study: Benjamin Franklin**: Franklin strategically built his reputation through public service, scientific achievements, and social networking. His focus on virtues such as frugality, industry, and humility helped him gain the trust and respect of his peers, ultimately leading to significant social and political influence.

- **Contemporary Case Study: Oprah Winfrey**: Oprah Winfrey's reputation for empathy, generosity, and integrity has played a crucial role in her success. By consistently promoting positive values and engaging in philanthropic activities, she has built a powerful personal brand that extends beyond her financial achievements.

3.5 The Impact and Outcomes of Reputation

The impact of reputation on wealth creation is profound. A strong reputation can lead to numerous benefits, including:

1. **Increased Trust and Cooperation**: Individuals with positive reputations are more likely to receive cooperation and support from others. This can lead to valuable partnerships, business opportunities, and social alliances.
2. **Attraction of Resources and Opportunities**: A good reputation can attract resources, such as investments, donations, and patronage. It can also open doors to new opportunities, such as leadership positions and influential networks.
3. **Protection Against Adversity**: A strong reputation can provide a buffer against negative events. For example, individuals with good reputations may receive support and protection during times of crisis, helping them recover more quickly.

Conclusion

Reputation and social capital are fundamental aspects of human social behaviour, deeply rooted in evolutionary psychology. Understanding the mechanisms behind reputation building and maintenance provides valuable insights into how individuals navigate social hierarchies and achieve success. By examining historical and contemporary examples, we can see how these principles continue to influence wealth creation and social dynamics in modern society.

Mating Strategies and Economic Behaviour

4.1 Sexual Selection and Resource Allocation

Sexual selection, a key component of evolutionary theory, explains how certain traits become more prevalent because they increase an individual's chances of successful mating. Resource allocation is closely tied to sexual selection, as resources can significantly enhance an individual's attractiveness as a mate.

In ancestral environments, individuals who could gather and control resources were more likely to attract mates. This principle still holds true today, as financial stability and resource availability are often considered desirable traits in potential partners. Research highlights how resource allocation strategies influence mate selection and reproductive success.

4.2 Mate Preferences and Wealth Indicators

Mate preferences have evolved to prioritise traits that signal resource availability and stability. These preferences can be observed across cultures and are deeply rooted in our evolutionary past. Several key indicators of wealth influence mate preferences:

1. **Economic Resources**: Wealth and financial stability are significant indicators of a desirable mate. Studies have shown that individuals with higher income levels are often preferred as partners due to their ability to provide security and support (Buss, 1989).

2. **Social Status**: High social status often correlates with increased access to resources. Individuals with high status are perceived as more attractive because they can provide better protection and opportunities for their offspring.
3. **Generosity**: Displays of generosity and altruism can enhance an individual's attractiveness. Generosity signals that an individual is willing to share resources, which can be beneficial for long-term partnerships and cooperative child-rearing.
4. **Ambition and Industriousness**: Traits such as ambition and industriousness are attractive because they indicate a potential for future resource acquisition. Partners who demonstrate these qualities are perceived as having a higher likelihood of achieving economic success.

4.3 Wealth as a Factor in Mate Choice

Wealth plays a critical role in mate choice, influencing both selection and competition. Individuals with substantial resources are often more successful in attracting and retaining mates. This dynamic can be understood through the lens of evolutionary psychology:

1. **Intersexual Selection**: This process involves individuals of one sex (typically females) selecting mates based on traits that indicate resource availability. Females often prioritise mates who can provide financial stability and

resources, which enhance the survival and reproductive success of their offspring.

2. **Intrasexual Competition**: Members of the same sex (typically males) compete for access to mates. Wealth and resources can give individuals a competitive edge in this process, as they can offer more to potential partners. This competition drives the accumulation and display of wealth as a means of attracting mates.

4.4 Evolutionary Case Studies on Wealth and Mating

To illustrate the principles of evolutionary psychology in mating strategies and economic behaviour, we can examine historical and contemporary case studies:

- **Historical Case Study: The Marriage Market in Victorian England**: During the Victorian era, marriage was often influenced by economic considerations. Families sought to marry their daughters to wealthy men to secure financial stability and social status. The exchange of dowries and the emphasis on wealth in marriage negotiations highlight the role of economic resources in mate selection.

- **Contemporary Case Study: Online Dating Platforms**: Modern dating platforms provide insights into mate preferences and economic behaviour. Research shows that profiles indicating higher income levels receive more attention and responses. This trend underscores the continued importance of financial stability in mate choice (Hitsch, Hortaçsu, & Ariely, 2010).

4.5 Implications for Wealth Accumulation

Understanding the link between mating strategies and economic behaviour has several implications for wealth accumulation:

1. **Motivation for Wealth**: The desire to attract and retain mates can drive individuals to accumulate wealth. This motivation is deeply rooted in our evolutionary history and continues to influence economic behaviour today.
2. **Resource Allocation**: How individuals allocate their resources can affect their attractiveness as mates. Investing in education, career development, and social status can enhance one's desirability and potential for forming successful partnerships.
3. **Long-Term Partnerships**: Wealth can contribute to the stability and success of long-term partnerships. Financial stability reduces stress and conflict in relationships, leading to better outcomes for couples and their offspring.

Conclusion

Mating strategies and economic behaviour are intricately linked, shaped by evolutionary pressures that prioritise resource availability and stability. By examining mate preferences and the role of wealth in mate choice, we gain a deeper understanding of how evolutionary psychology influences economic actions. These insights highlight the enduring impact of our evolutionary past on modern financial behaviour.

Parental Investment and
Wealth Transmission

5.1 The Evolution of Parental Investment

Parental investment theory, formulated by Robert Trivers, posits that the energy, time, and resources parents devote to their offspring can significantly influence the survival and reproductive success of their children. From an evolutionary standpoint, the extent of parental investment varies across species, but in humans, substantial investment is critical for offspring survival and success.

In human societies, parental investment includes providing food, shelter, education, and social connections. These resources enhance a child's ability to thrive and compete in their social environment. The evolutionary basis for this investment is clear: parents who invest more in their offspring increase the likelihood that their genes will be passed on to future generations.

5.2 Strategies for Wealth Transmission

Wealth transmission is an extension of parental investment, where parents aim to provide their offspring with a secure and advantageous starting point in life. There are several strategies for effective wealth transmission:

1. **Direct Financial Transfers**: This involves the transfer of money or assets directly to offspring. Inheritance, gifts, and trust funds are common methods. Direct financial transfers can provide

immediate benefits but may also come with challenges such as inheritance taxes and the potential for mismanagement.

2. **Education and Skills Development**: Investing in education and skill acquisition is a long-term strategy for wealth transmission. By ensuring that their children receive quality education and develop valuable skills, parents increase their offspring's potential for economic success and independence.

3. **Social Capital**: Building and maintaining social networks is another crucial strategy. Parents can transmit social capital by introducing their children to influential networks and fostering connections that can provide opportunities and support.

4. **Values and Norms**: Instilling values such as hard work, financial responsibility, and ethical behaviour can also be considered a form of wealth transmission. These values help children manage and grow their inherited wealth effectively.

5.3 The Role of Kin Selection

Kin selection theory, another concept developed by Robert Trivers, explains how behaviours that seem altruistic can actually increase an individual's genetic fitness by benefiting relatives. In the context of wealth transmission, kin selection plays a significant role.

Parents are biologically inclined to favour their offspring in wealth transmission. This inclination ensures that their genetic material has a better chance of surviving and reproducing. However, wealth transmission can extend beyond direct offspring to other relatives, such as nieces, nephews, and grandchildren, especially in cultures where extended family ties are strong.

5.4 Cultural Variations in Inheritance

Inheritance practices vary widely across cultures, reflecting different societal norms, legal frameworks, and economic systems. These variations influence how wealth is transmitted and perceived:

1. **Primogeniture**: In many historical and some contemporary societies, primogeniture—the practice of passing wealth primarily to the eldest son—has been common. This practice ensures the continuity of family wealth and status but can create disparities among siblings.
2. **Equal Inheritance**: In contrast, many modern societies promote equal inheritance among children, reflecting values of fairness and equality. This practice can help prevent family conflict and ensure that all offspring have similar opportunities.
3. **Matrilineal and Patrilineal Systems**: Some cultures follow matrilineal inheritance, where wealth is passed through the female line, while others follow patrilineal systems, where wealth is

transmitted through the male line. These systems are often tied to broader social and economic structures.

4. **Cultural Case Study: The Akan of Ghana**: The Akan people of Ghana follow a matrilineal system of inheritance. Wealth and social status are passed through the mother's lineage, ensuring that women play a central role in the transmission of wealth and power (Sarpong, 1974).

5.5 Evolutionary Implications of Wealth Transmission

The strategies and cultural practices surrounding wealth transmission have significant evolutionary implications. Effective wealth transmission enhances the survival and reproductive success of offspring, ensuring that the family's genetic legacy continues. However, the methods of transmission can also create social dynamics that influence broader societal structures.

For example, unequal inheritance practices can lead to social stratification, where wealth and power are concentrated in certain families or social groups. This stratification can influence mate selection, social alliances, and competition for resources, perpetuating cycles of wealth and poverty across generations.

Conclusion

Parental investment and wealth transmission are deeply rooted in evolutionary biology and play crucial roles in human social dynamics. By understanding the strategies and cultural practices associated with wealth transmission, we gain insights into how parents ensure the success of their offspring and how these practices shape broader societal patterns. The interplay between biology and culture in wealth transmission highlights the complexity of human economic behaviour and its evolutionary underpinnings.

Social Alliances and
Wealth Preservation

6.1 The Evolution of Social Alliances

Social alliances have been a critical aspect of human survival and success. From an evolutionary perspective, forming and maintaining alliances provided individuals with protection, resources, and support. These alliances were essential for survival in ancestral environments where solitary living was fraught with dangers.

Evolutionary psychology explains that humans are naturally predisposed to form alliances because they offer significant adaptive advantages. Alliances can enhance an individual's status, increase access to resources, and provide support in times of need. The same principles that governed alliances in ancestral environments apply to modern economic and social contexts.

6.2 Reciprocity and Trust in Wealth Management

Reciprocity and trust are foundational elements of successful social alliances. These principles are rooted in evolutionary biology, where reciprocal altruism— exchanging benefits with the expectation of future returns—plays a vital role in cooperation.

1. **Reciprocity**: This involves a mutual exchange of resources or services. In economic terms, reciprocity can be seen in business partnerships, trade agreements, and social networks where individuals and organisations help each other with the expectation of future benefits.

2. **Trust**: Trust is crucial for maintaining long-term alliances. It reduces the uncertainty in interactions and fosters cooperation. Evolutionary psychology suggests that trust is built through repeated interactions and consistent behaviour, creating a reputation for reliability and fairness.

Studies have shown that trust and reciprocity are critical in economic transactions. For example, research in behavioural economics highlights that individuals are more likely to engage in financial exchanges with those they trust, which leads to more stable and productive economic relationships (Fehr & Fischbacher, 2003).

6.3 Strategies for Conflict Resolution

Conflict is inevitable in social and economic interactions, but effective conflict resolution strategies are essential for preserving wealth and maintaining alliances. Evolutionary psychology offers insights into conflict resolution mechanisms that have evolved to minimise harm and maximise cooperation.

1. **Mediation and Negotiation**: These strategies involve third parties or direct discussions to resolve conflicts. Mediation helps parties reach a mutually acceptable solution, while negotiation allows for the exchange of concessions to achieve a beneficial outcome.

2. **Reputation Management**: Maintaining a good reputation can help prevent conflicts and facilitate their resolution. Individuals and organisations with strong reputations for fairness and integrity are more likely to resolve disputes amicably.

3. **Social Sanctions**: In some cases, social sanctions—such as ostracism or public criticism—can be used to enforce cooperative behaviour and resolve conflicts. These sanctions can deter individuals from engaging in harmful actions and encourage adherence to social norms.

6.4 Alliances in Historical and Modern Contexts

Historical and contemporary examples illustrate the importance of social alliances in wealth preservation:

- **Historical Case Study: The Hanseatic League**: The Hanseatic League was a commercial and defensive confederation of merchant guilds and market towns in Northwestern and Central Europe. Founded in the late 12th century, it facilitated trade and protected economic interests through mutual cooperation and alliances. The league's success highlights the power of economic alliances in wealth preservation.

- **Contemporary Case Study: The Business Networks of Silicon Valley**: Silicon Valley is renowned for its vibrant ecosystem of entrepreneurs, investors, and corporations. The success of many companies in Silicon Valley can be attributed to the strong network of alliances and collaborative culture. These networks provide access to resources, expertise, and support, facilitating innovation and wealth creation.

6.5 The Role of Social Hierarchies in Wealth Preservation

Social hierarchies play a significant role in the formation and maintenance of alliances. Hierarchies help organise social groups and determine the distribution of resources and responsibilities. In both ancestral and modern contexts, individuals who occupy higher positions in social hierarchies have better access to resources and opportunities.

1. **Status and Influence**: High-status individuals often have greater influence in forming and maintaining alliances. Their status can attract allies and deter competitors, enhancing their ability to preserve and grow wealth.
2. **Resource Control**: Those at the top of social hierarchies typically control more resources, which they can use to reinforce their position and support their allies. This control can create a positive feedback loop, where wealth and status mutually reinforce each other.

6.6 Cooperative Strategies in Economic Behaviour

Cooperation is a cornerstone of economic behaviour. Evolutionary psychology explains that humans have evolved to cooperate because it offers significant adaptive benefits. Cooperative strategies can enhance wealth preservation by pooling resources, sharing risks, and fostering innovation.

1. **Joint Ventures and Partnerships**: These arrangements allow organisations to combine their strengths and resources to achieve common goals. Joint ventures can lead to increased efficiency, innovation, and market reach.
2. **Collective Investment**: Collective investment schemes, such as mutual funds and investment clubs, enable individuals to pool their resources for greater financial returns. This cooperation can reduce risks and provide access to investment opportunities that might be unavailable to individuals.
3. **Collaborative Innovation**: Innovation often results from collaborative efforts. By working together, individuals and organisations can combine their knowledge and resources to develop new products, services, and technologies.

Conclusion

Social alliances and cooperative strategies are essential for wealth preservation and economic success. By understanding the evolutionary principles that underpin these behaviours, we can better navigate the complexities of modern economic interactions. Historical and contemporary examples demonstrate the enduring importance of alliances and cooperation in achieving long-term wealth preservation.

Risk-Taking and Innovation

7.1 The Evolutionary Basis of Risk-Taking

Risk-taking is a behaviour deeply rooted in our evolutionary past. In ancestral environments, taking risks could lead to significant rewards, such as securing food, territory, or mates. However, it also came with potential costs, including injury or death. Evolutionary psychology explains that individuals who were able to successfully navigate these risks often had a competitive advantage, leading to greater survival and reproductive success.

Research by evolutionary psychologists highlights that risk-taking behaviours are influenced by several factors, such as age, gender, and social context. For instance, young males are generally more likely to engage in risk-taking behaviours, which can be attributed to sexual selection pressures where demonstrating bravery and resourcefulness could enhance their attractiveness to potential mates.

7.2 Innovation and Wealth Creation

Innovation is closely linked to risk-taking. The willingness to take risks often drives individuals to explore new ideas, technologies, and strategies that can lead to significant economic gains. Throughout history, many of the greatest innovations have come from individuals who were willing to challenge the status quo and take substantial risks.

1. **Technological Innovation**: Technological advancements have been a primary driver of

wealth creation. Innovators like Thomas Edison and Steve Jobs took significant risks in developing new technologies that transformed industries and created enormous economic value.

2. **Entrepreneurial Ventures**: Entrepreneurship involves significant risk-taking, as new ventures often face high uncertainty and potential for failure. However, successful entrepreneurs, such as Elon Musk and Richard Branson, have demonstrated that calculated risk-taking can lead to substantial wealth accumulation and societal impact.

7.3 The Psychology of Risk and Reward

Understanding the psychological mechanisms behind risk-taking can provide insights into economic behaviour and innovation. Several cognitive and emotional factors influence risk-taking decisions:

1. **Risk Perception**: How individuals perceive risk can vary based on their experiences, knowledge, and cognitive biases. Some may underestimate risks due to overconfidence, while others may overestimate them due to fear of loss.

2. **Reward Sensitivity**: The brain's reward system, particularly the role of neurotransmitters like dopamine, plays a crucial role in risk-taking behaviour. Individuals with higher reward sensitivity are more likely to pursue high-risk, high-reward opportunities.

3. **Loss Aversion**: The concept of loss aversion, introduced by behavioural economists Daniel Kahneman and Amos Tversky, explains that individuals tend to prefer avoiding losses over acquiring equivalent gains. This can influence risk-taking behaviour, often making individuals more conservative in their decisions (Kahneman & Tversky, 1979).

7.4 Case Studies of Successful Innovators

Examining the lives and careers of successful innovators can provide valuable insights into the role of risk-taking in wealth creation:

- **Historical Case Study: Nikola Tesla**: Tesla was a pioneer in electrical engineering and a prolific inventor. Despite facing numerous challenges and setbacks, his willingness to take risks and pursue unconventional ideas led to groundbreaking innovations in alternating current (AC) electricity and wireless communication.
- **Contemporary Case Study: Jeff Bezos**: As the founder of Amazon, Jeff Bezos took significant risks by leaving a secure job and investing in a nascent e-commerce industry. His long-term vision and risk-taking approach enabled Amazon to grow from an online bookstore into one of the world's largest and most diversified companies.

7.5 Balancing Risk and Stability

While risk-taking is essential for innovation and wealth creation, it is equally important to balance risk with stability. Excessive risk-taking can lead to significant losses, while an overly conservative approach can stifle innovation and growth. Successful individuals and organisations often adopt strategies to manage and mitigate risks:

1. **Diversification**: Diversifying investments and ventures can spread risk across different areas, reducing the impact of potential losses. This strategy is commonly used in financial portfolios and business operations.
2. **Incremental Innovation**: Instead of pursuing radical changes, some innovators focus on incremental improvements. This approach allows for steady progress and reduces the risks associated with major disruptions.
3. **Contingency Planning**: Preparing for potential setbacks and having contingency plans in place can help manage risks effectively. This includes financial reserves, alternative strategies, and crisis management plans.

Conclusion

Risk-taking and innovation are fundamental drivers of wealth creation. Understanding the evolutionary basis of these behaviours provides valuable insights into how individuals and organisations can navigate uncertainties and seize opportunities. By balancing risk with stability and learning from successful innovators, we can foster an environment that encourages creativity, resilience, and long-term economic growth.

Competition and
Cooperation

8.1 Evolutionary Perspectives on Competition

Competition is a fundamental aspect of human behaviour, deeply rooted in our evolutionary past. In ancestral environments, individuals competed for limited resources such as food, shelter, and mates. This competition was crucial for survival and reproductive success. Evolutionary psychology explains that competitive behaviours have been shaped by natural selection to enhance an individual's chances of obtaining resources and passing on their genes.

Evolutionary psychologists have identified several key drivers of competition:

1. **Scarcity of Resources**: Limited availability of resources necessitates competition.
2. **Reproductive Success**: Competing for mates ensures the continuation of one's genetic lineage.
3. **Social Status**: Higher social status often correlates with better access to resources and mating opportunities.

8.2 Cooperative Strategies in Wealth Building

While competition is essential, cooperation is equally vital for human success. Cooperative behaviours allow individuals to pool resources, share risks, and work together towards common goals. Evolutionary psychology highlights several mechanisms that promote cooperation:

1. **Reciprocal Altruism**: This principle, proposed by Robert Trivers, suggests that individuals engage in cooperative behaviours with the expectation that the favour will be returned in the future. This creates a mutually beneficial relationship that enhances survival and success.
2. **Kin Selection**: Helping relatives can increase the likelihood of one's genes being passed on, even if it involves personal sacrifices. This principle explains why individuals are often more willing to cooperate with family members (Hamilton, 1964).
3. **Group Selection**: Groups that exhibit cooperative behaviours are more likely to survive and prosper compared to those that do not. This selection pressure promotes the evolution of traits that enhance group cohesion and cooperation (Wilson, 1975).

8.3 Balancing Competition and Cooperation

Balancing competition and cooperation is crucial for wealth building and social harmony. While competition drives innovation and individual success, cooperation fosters collective well-being and stability. Successful individuals and organisations often strike a balance between these two strategies to achieve long-term success.

1. **Collaborative Competition**: This approach involves competing within a framework of

cooperation. For example, companies in a collaborative ecosystem can compete in the marketplace while working together on common goals such as industry standards and research initiatives.

2. **Coopetition**: A blend of cooperation and competition, where businesses cooperate in certain areas while competing in others. This strategy allows companies to leverage each other's strengths and resources while maintaining competitive dynamics.

3. **Strategic Alliances**: Forming alliances with competitors can lead to mutually beneficial outcomes. These alliances can include joint ventures, research collaborations, and cross-industry partnerships.

8.4 Case Studies of Competition and Cooperation

Examining historical and contemporary examples provides insights into how competition and cooperation shape economic behaviour:

- **Historical Case Study: The Rivalry Between Tesla and Edison**: The competition between Nikola Tesla and Thomas Edison over the development of electrical power systems was intense. While their rivalry spurred significant technological advancements, both inventors also relied on cooperation with investors, companies, and other scientists to achieve their goals.

- **Contemporary Case Study: The Tech Industry in Silicon Valley**: Silicon Valley exemplifies the balance between competition and cooperation. Companies fiercely compete for market share, talent, and innovation. Simultaneously, they engage in cooperative initiatives such as open-source projects, industry consortia, and collaborative research.

8.5 Competitive Dynamics in Economic Behaviour

Understanding the dynamics of competition can provide valuable insights into economic behaviour:

1. **Market Competition**: In economic markets, competition drives efficiency, innovation, and consumer choice. Companies strive to outperform each other by developing better products, reducing costs, and enhancing customer experiences.
2. **Workplace Competition**: Within organisations, employees often compete for promotions, recognition, and rewards. This competition can motivate individuals to perform at their best, contributing to overall organisational success.
3. **Global Competition**: On a global scale, countries compete for economic dominance, technological leadership, and geopolitical influence. This competition can lead to advancements in technology, infrastructure, and standards of living.

8.6 Cooperative Dynamics in Economic Behaviour

Cooperation also plays a crucial role in economic behaviour:

1. **Trade and Commerce**: International trade relies on cooperation between countries, enabling the exchange of goods, services, and capital. Trade agreements and economic partnerships foster global economic growth and interdependence.
2. **Corporate Social Responsibility**: Companies increasingly recognise the importance of cooperating with stakeholders, including employees, communities, and governments. Corporate social responsibility initiatives promote sustainable practices, social welfare, and ethical business conduct.
3. **Collaborative Innovation**: Innovation often results from collaborative efforts. By working together, individuals and organisations can combine their knowledge and resources to develop new products, services, and technologies.

Conclusion

Competition and cooperation are fundamental aspects of human economic behaviour, shaped by evolutionary pressures. Understanding the balance between these two strategies provides valuable insights into wealth building and social dynamics. By examining historical and contemporary examples, we can appreciate the complex interplay between competition and cooperation in shaping human success.

Psychological Mechanisms
of Wealth Perception

9.1 Cognitive Biases and Financial Decisions

Human decision-making is heavily influenced by cognitive biases—systematic patterns of deviation from norm or rationality in judgment. These biases are rooted in our evolutionary past, where quick, heuristic-based decisions often meant the difference between life and death. In modern financial contexts, these biases can significantly impact wealth perception and management.

1. **Overconfidence Bias**: Overconfidence is a common bias where individuals overestimate their knowledge or abilities. This bias can lead to excessive risk-taking in financial decisions, as people believe they are more capable of predicting market movements or managing investments than they actually are (Barber & Odean, 2001).

2. **Loss Aversion**: Loss aversion, identified by Kahneman and Tversky, describes the tendency for people to prefer avoiding losses over acquiring equivalent gains. This bias can lead to overly conservative financial behaviour, as the fear of losing money outweighs the potential benefits of higher-risk investments (Kahneman & Tversky, 1979).

3. **Anchoring**: Anchoring occurs when individuals rely too heavily on the first piece of information they encounter (the "anchor") when making decisions. In financial contexts, this can result in mispricing assets or failing to adjust expectations

based on new information (Tversky & Kahneman, 1974).

4. **Herd Behaviour**: Herd behaviour describes how individuals in a group can act collectively without centralised direction. In financial markets, this can lead to phenomena such as bubbles and crashes, as investors follow the crowd rather than making independent assessments.

9.2 The Role of Emotions in Wealth Management

Emotions play a significant role in financial decision-making. While traditional economic theories often assume rational behaviour, real-world decisions are frequently influenced by emotional responses.

1. **Fear and Greed**: These two emotions are powerful drivers in financial markets. Fear can lead to panic selling during market downturns, while greed can drive speculative bubbles during market upswings.

2. **Regret and Pride**: The anticipation of regret can influence decision-making, leading individuals to avoid actions that might result in future regret. Conversely, the desire for pride can motivate individuals to take actions that will result in personal or social recognition.

3. **Emotional Contagion**: Emotions can spread through social networks, influencing group behaviour. For example, widespread fear during

a financial crisis can lead to collective selling, exacerbating market declines.

9.3 Perception of Wealth and Social Status

Wealth is not just a measure of financial assets; it is also a significant determinant of social status. The perception of wealth can influence an individual's social standing and how they are treated by others.

1. **Conspicuous Consumption**: As proposed by Thorstein Veblen, conspicuous consumption involves spending on luxury goods and services to display economic power and enhance social status. This behaviour is driven by the desire to signal wealth and status to others (Veblen, 1899).
2. **Relative Wealth**: People often judge their wealth relative to others. This social comparison can influence financial satisfaction and decision-making. For instance, individuals may feel wealthy if they perceive themselves as better off than their peers, even if their absolute wealth is modest.
3. **Cultural Variations**: Different cultures have varying attitudes towards wealth and status. In some cultures, modesty and humility are valued, while in others, displaying wealth is a sign of success and power.

9.4 Strategies to Optimise Decision-Making

Understanding cognitive biases and emotional influences can help individuals make better financial decisions. Here are some strategies to optimise wealth management:

1. **Education and Awareness**: Increasing awareness of common cognitive biases can help individuals recognise and mitigate their effects. Financial education programs can teach people about the psychological pitfalls of investing and decision-making.

2. **Decision Frameworks**: Using structured decision-making frameworks, such as checklists and decision trees, can reduce the influence of biases and emotions. These tools help ensure that decisions are based on rational analysis rather than impulsive reactions.

3. **Diversification**: Diversifying investments can help manage risk and reduce the impact of biased decision-making. By spreading investments across different asset classes, individuals can protect themselves against the volatility of any single investment.

4. **Emotional Regulation**: Developing strategies to manage emotions, such as mindfulness and stress-reduction techniques, can improve financial decision-making. By staying calm and focused, individuals are less likely to make impulsive or emotionally-driven choices.

9.5 Case Studies on Wealth Perception and Decision-Making

Examining real-world examples provides valuable insights into the psychological mechanisms of wealth perception:

- **Case Study: The Dot-Com Bubble**: The late 1990s saw a massive surge in technology stock prices, driven by overconfidence, herd behaviour, and the fear of missing out. When the bubble burst, many investors faced significant losses, highlighting the dangers of biased decision-making and emotional investing.
- **Case Study: The 2008 Financial Crisis**: The global financial crisis was exacerbated by cognitive biases such as overconfidence in the housing market and herd behaviour in mortgage-backed securities. The emotional reactions of fear and panic led to widespread selling and market declines.

Conclusion

Cognitive biases and emotional influences are integral to understanding financial decision-making and wealth perception. By recognising these psychological mechanisms, individuals can develop strategies to optimise their financial decisions and manage their wealth more effectively. The interplay between cognitive biases, emotions, and social status underscores the complexity of human economic behaviour and its evolutionary roots.

Cultural Evolution and Economic Systems

10.1 The Co-Evolution of Culture and Economics

Culture and economics are intricately linked, co-evolving over time. Culture encompasses the beliefs, values, norms, and practices that characterise a society, while economics deals with the production, distribution, and consumption of goods and services. From an evolutionary perspective, these two domains influence each other in significant ways.

Cultural evolution refers to the process by which cultural traits change over time through mechanisms such as transmission, variation, and selection. Just as biological traits evolve through natural selection, cultural traits evolve based on their impact on the survival and reproductive success of individuals and groups.

10.2 Impact of Cultural Norms on Wealth Distribution

Cultural norms significantly influence how wealth is distributed and perceived within a society. These norms can shape economic behaviours, social hierarchies, and the overall functioning of economic systems.

1. **Individualism vs. Collectivism**: In individualistic cultures, personal achievement and wealth accumulation are highly valued, leading to economic systems that emphasise competition and individual success. In contrast, collectivist cultures prioritise group harmony and shared

wealth, often resulting in more cooperative economic practices.

2. **Attitudes Toward Wealth**: Cultural attitudes towards wealth can vary widely. Some cultures view wealth accumulation positively, associating it with success and hard work. Others may emphasise modesty and view excessive wealth as a sign of greed or moral corruption.

3. **Economic Inequality**: Cultural norms also affect perceptions of economic inequality. Societies with strong egalitarian values may implement policies to redistribute wealth and reduce disparities, while those with hierarchical norms may accept or even reinforce economic inequalities.

10.3 Comparative Analysis of Different Economic Systems

Examining different economic systems through the lens of cultural evolution provides insights into how cultural traits influence economic structures and outcomes.

1. **Capitalism**: Capitalism, characterised by private ownership and free markets, thrives in cultures that value individualism, innovation, and competition. The United States is a prime example, where the cultural emphasis on personal freedom and entrepreneurship supports a dynamic capitalist economy.

2. **Socialism**: Socialism, which emphasises collective ownership and wealth redistribution, aligns with cultures that prioritise equality and social welfare. Scandinavian countries like Sweden and Denmark exemplify this system, where strong social safety nets and wealth redistribution policies reflect cultural values of social equity and solidarity.

3. **Mixed Economies**: Many countries operate mixed economies, combining elements of capitalism and socialism. These systems reflect a balance between individual initiative and social welfare, influenced by cultural norms that value both personal freedom and social responsibility. Examples include Canada and Germany, where market-driven economies coexist with robust public services.

10.4 Cultural Case Studies

Cultural case studies illustrate the diverse ways in which cultural evolution shapes economic systems and wealth distribution:

- **Case Study: Japan**: Japan's economic system reflects its collectivist culture, which values group harmony, social cohesion, and long-term relationships. Despite being a capitalist economy, Japan places significant emphasis on corporate loyalty, lifetime employment, and social stability. These cultural traits have influenced business practices and economic policies, contributing to Japan's unique economic landscape.

- **Case Study: The United Arab Emirates**: The UAE's rapid economic development is rooted in its cultural adaptation to global capitalism while maintaining traditional values. The country leverages its oil wealth to diversify its economy and invest in infrastructure, tourism, and finance. Cultural values of hospitality, respect for authority, and strategic vision drive the UAE's economic policies and international partnerships.

10.5 Future Directions in Wealth and Culture

As the world becomes increasingly interconnected, cultural and economic systems continue to evolve. Understanding the interplay between cultural evolution and economic systems can provide insights into future trends and challenges.

1. **Globalisation**: Globalisation accelerates the exchange of cultural and economic practices across borders. While it can lead to cultural homogenisation, it also fosters innovation and economic growth by introducing new ideas and technologies.
2. **Technological Advancements**: Technology influences cultural and economic evolution by shaping communication, production, and

consumption patterns. The rise of the digital economy, for example, is transforming traditional business models and creating new opportunities for wealth generation.

3. **Sustainability and Social Responsibility**: There is a growing cultural shift towards sustainability and social responsibility. Economic systems are increasingly incorporating environmental and social considerations, driven by cultural values that prioritise long-term well-being and ethical behaviour.

4. **Cultural Adaptation**: Societies continuously adapt their cultural and economic practices to changing environments. This adaptive capacity is crucial for addressing global challenges such as climate change, economic inequality, and social justice.

Conclusion

Cultural evolution and economic systems are deeply intertwined, shaping how societies accumulate, distribute, and perceive wealth. By examining the co-evolution of culture and economics, we gain a deeper understanding of the diverse ways in which cultural traits influence economic behaviour and outcomes. This perspective highlights the importance of cultural context in shaping economic policies and practices, providing valuable insights for navigating the complexities of the modern world.

Wealth, Health, and Longevity

11.1 The Interconnection Between Wealth and Health

Wealth and health are deeply interconnected, with numerous studies demonstrating that higher levels of wealth are associated with better health outcomes and increased longevity. From an evolutionary perspective, the resources provided by wealth can improve an individual's capacity to survive and reproduce.

Wealth can enhance health in several ways:

1. **Access to Medical Care**: Wealthier individuals can afford better healthcare, including preventative care, early diagnosis, and advanced treatments.
2. **Nutrition**: Wealth allows for the purchase of healthier foods and nutritional supplements, which are crucial for maintaining good health.
3. **Living Conditions**: Wealthy individuals typically live in safer, cleaner environments that reduce the risk of illness and injury.
4. **Stress Reduction**: Financial security can reduce stress, which is linked to numerous health problems, including heart disease, anxiety, and depression.

11.2 Evolutionary Perspectives on Wealth and Longevity

Evolutionary psychology provides insights into why wealth influences health and longevity. Resources have always been critical for survival and reproductive success. In ancestral environments, individuals with better access to resources were more likely to survive harsh conditions, recover from illnesses, and attract mates.

1. **Parental Investment**: Wealth enables greater parental investment in offspring, improving their chances of survival and success. This investment includes better healthcare, nutrition, education, and social opportunities.
2. **Mate Selection**: Wealth signals genetic fitness and resource availability, making wealthy individuals more attractive as mates. This preference is rooted in the evolutionary benefits of partnering with resource-rich individuals who can provide for offspring.
3. **Social Status**: Higher social status, often associated with wealth, can lead to better health outcomes due to reduced stress and increased access to social and economic resources.

11.3 Strategies for Maintaining Health Through Wealth

Wealth can be strategically used to maintain and improve health, thus extending longevity:

1. **Preventative Healthcare**: Investing in regular health check-ups, vaccinations, and preventative screenings can detect health issues early and prevent serious illnesses.
2. **Healthy Lifestyle Choices**: Wealth allows for investments in fitness programs, healthy diets,

and wellness retreats. These choices contribute to long-term health and well-being.

3. **Mental Health**: Wealth can provide access to mental health resources, such as therapy, stress management programs, and mindfulness practices. Maintaining mental health is crucial for overall well-being and longevity.

4. **Social Engagement**: Wealth can facilitate social connections and activities that promote mental and emotional health. Engaging in community events, clubs, and social gatherings can reduce feelings of isolation and depression.

11.4 Case Studies on Wealth and Longevity

Examining real-world examples can illustrate the impact of wealth on health and longevity:

- **Case Study: The Rockefeller Family**: The Rockefellers are one of the wealthiest families in American history. Their wealth has allowed them to access the best medical care, nutrition, and living conditions, contributing to their longevity. Many members of the Rockefeller family have lived into their 90s, exemplifying the connection between wealth and health.

- **Case Study: The Blue Zones**: Blue Zones are regions where people live significantly longer lives. While not all Blue Zones are wealthy, they often share traits such as strong social connections, healthy diets, and active lifestyles.

Wealthier Blue Zone residents can enhance these traits through better healthcare and living conditions.

11.5 Evolutionary Strategies for Future Generations

Understanding the evolutionary basis of wealth and health can help develop strategies to enhance longevity for future generations:

1. **Investment in Education**: Educating future generations about the importance of health and financial management can empower them to make informed decisions that promote well-being and longevity.
2. **Sustainable Practices**: Investing in sustainable practices ensures that future generations have access to clean air, water, and food, which are essential for health.
3. **Advancements in Healthcare**: Continued investment in medical research and healthcare innovations can improve disease prevention, diagnosis, and treatment, extending healthy lifespans.
4. **Social Policies**: Advocating for social policies that promote equal access to healthcare, education, and economic opportunities can help reduce health disparities and improve overall societal health.

Conclusion

The interconnection between wealth, health, and longevity underscores the importance of financial resources in promoting well-being and extending life. By understanding the evolutionary perspectives and leveraging wealth strategically, individuals can enhance their health and longevity. Future generations can benefit from these insights through education, sustainable practices, healthcare advancements, and supportive social policies.

The Future of Wealth in an Evolutionary Context

12.1 Predicting Future Trends in Wealth Accumulation

Understanding the evolutionary underpinnings of wealth accumulation provides a foundation for predicting future trends. As society evolves, technological advancements, demographic changes, and cultural shifts will continue to influence how wealth is created and distributed.

1. **Technological Innovation**: Advances in technology, such as artificial intelligence, blockchain, and biotechnology, will open new avenues for wealth creation. These technologies can lead to increased productivity, new industries, and innovative business models. However, they may also disrupt traditional job markets and exacerbate economic inequalities.

2. **Globalisation**: The interconnectedness of global economies will continue to influence wealth dynamics. While globalisation can lead to economic growth and increased access to markets, it can also result in uneven wealth distribution and increased competition for resources.

3. **Demographic Shifts**: Changes in population dynamics, such as aging populations in developed countries and youthful demographics in developing nations, will impact economic systems. These shifts will influence labour markets, social security systems, and investment opportunities.

12.2 The Impact of Technological Advancements

Technological advancements have historically driven significant changes in wealth accumulation and distribution. Future technologies will likely continue this trend, presenting both opportunities and challenges.

1. **Automation and AI**: Automation and artificial intelligence can increase efficiency and productivity, leading to economic growth. However, they also pose the risk of job displacement and increased income inequality. Policies and strategies to retrain and reskill the workforce will be crucial in mitigating these impacts.
2. **Blockchain and Cryptocurrencies**: Blockchain technology and cryptocurrencies have the potential to revolutionise financial systems by providing decentralised, transparent, and secure ways to conduct transactions. They can enhance financial inclusion and reduce transaction costs but also pose regulatory and security challenges.
3. **Biotechnology and Health**: Advances in biotechnology can lead to new medical treatments and improved healthcare outcomes, enhancing longevity and quality of life. These advancements can create significant economic value but may also raise ethical and accessibility concerns.

12.3 Evolutionary Strategies for Future Generations

To ensure future generations can navigate the evolving economic landscape, it is essential to apply evolutionary strategies that have proven effective over time.

1. **Adaptability and Resilience**: Encouraging adaptability and resilience will help individuals and societies manage change and uncertainty. This involves fostering a mindset of continuous learning, flexibility, and innovation.
2. **Investment in Education and Skills**: Investing in education and skills development is critical for preparing future generations for the demands of a rapidly changing economy. Emphasising STEM (science, technology, engineering, and mathematics) education, as well as soft skills like critical thinking and emotional intelligence, will be crucial.
3. **Sustainable Practices**: Emphasising sustainability in economic activities can ensure long-term resource availability and environmental health. This includes adopting practices that reduce waste, conserve resources, and promote renewable energy.
4. **Inclusive Policies**: Implementing policies that promote economic inclusion and reduce inequality can enhance social stability and cohesion. This includes progressive taxation, social safety nets, and initiatives to support marginalised communities.

12.4 Cultural Evolution and Wealth

Cultural evolution will continue to shape economic behaviours and systems. Understanding how cultural traits influence wealth accumulation can provide insights into future economic trends.

1. **Shifts in Work Culture**: The traditional 9-to-5 work model may evolve into more flexible and remote work arrangements. This shift can influence productivity, work-life balance, and economic participation.
2. **Changing Attitudes Towards Wealth**: Cultural attitudes towards wealth and consumption may shift towards sustainability and social responsibility. As awareness of environmental and social issues grows, consumers and investors may prioritise ethical and sustainable practices.
3. **Global Cultural Exchange**: Increased cultural exchange and diversity can lead to the blending of economic practices and the adoption of innovative approaches to wealth creation and management.

12.5 Case Studies of Future-Oriented Wealth Strategies

Examining forward-thinking individuals and organisations can provide valuable lessons for future wealth strategies:

- **Case Study: Elon Musk and SpaceX**: Elon Musk's ventures, particularly SpaceX, exemplify the integration of technological innovation, risk-taking, and long-term vision. SpaceX's advancements in space technology and reusable rockets have the potential to revolutionise space exploration and create new economic opportunities.

- **Case Study: The Rise of Impact Investing**: Impact investing focuses on generating positive social and environmental outcomes alongside financial returns. This approach reflects a growing trend towards aligning investment strategies with broader societal goals. Companies and funds that prioritise sustainability, social responsibility, and ethical governance are gaining traction among investors.

12.6 Concluding Thoughts on Wealth and Evolution

Wealth creation and accumulation are deeply influenced by evolutionary principles. As society continues to evolve, understanding these principles can provide valuable insights into navigating future economic landscapes. By applying strategies that emphasise adaptability, innovation, sustainability, and inclusivity, individuals and societies can build resilient and prosperous futures.

Key Takeaways

- **Evolutionary Insights**: Evolutionary psychology offers a framework for understanding wealth-related behaviours and strategies.

- **Technological Impact**: Embracing technological advancements can drive economic growth while addressing potential disruptions.
- **Cultural Adaptation**: Adapting cultural norms and practices to align with changing economic realities can enhance wealth creation and distribution.
- **Future Strategies**: Fostering adaptability, investing in education, promoting sustainability, and implementing inclusive policies are critical for future success.

Bibliography

Barber, B. M., & Odean, T. (2001). Boys Will Be Boys: Gender, Overconfidence, and Common Stock Investment. Quarterly Journal of Economics, 116(1), 261-292.

Buss, D. M. (1989). Sex Differences in Human Mate Preferences: Evolutionary Hypotheses Tested in 37 Cultures. Behavioral and Brain Sciences, 12(1), 1-49.

Buss, D. M. (2019). Evolutionary Psychology: The New Science of the Mind (5th ed.). Routledge.

Fehr, E., & Fischbacher, U. (2003). The nature of human altruism. Nature, 425(6960), 785-791.

Hamilton, W. D. (1964). The Genetical Evolution of Social Behavior. I & II. Journal of Theoretical Biology, 7(1), 1-52.

Harari, Y. N. (2015). Sapiens: A Brief History of Humankind. Harper.

Hitsch, G. J., Hortaçsu, A., & Ariely, D. (2010). Matching and Sorting in Online Dating. American Economic Review, 100(1), 130-163.

Hofstede, G. (2001). Culture's Consequences: Comparing Values, Behaviors, Institutions, and Organizations Across Nations. Sage Publications.

Inglehart, R., & Baker, W. E. (2000). Modernization, Cultural Change, and the Persistence of Traditional Values. American Sociological Review, 65(1), 19-51.

Kahneman, D., & Tversky, A. (1979). Prospect Theory: An Analysis of Decision under Risk. Econometrica, 47(2), 263-291.

Marmot, M. G., & Wilkinson, R. G. (2005). Social Determinants of Health. Oxford University Press.

Sarpong, P. (1974). Ghana in Retrospect: Some Aspects of Ghanaian Culture. Accra: Ghana Publishing Corporation.

Sapolsky, R. M. (2004). Why Zebras Don't Get Ulcers: The Acclaimed Guide to Stress, Stress-Related Diseases, and Coping. Henry Holt and Co.

Schwab, K. (2016). The Fourth Industrial Revolution. World Economic Forum.

Tomasello, M. (2009). Why We Cooperate. MIT Press.

Trivers, R. L. (1971). The Evolution of Reciprocal Altruism. Quarterly Review of Biology, 46(1), 35-57.

Trivers, R. L. (1972). Parental Investment and Sexual Selection. In B. Campbell (Ed.), Sexual Selection and the Descent of Man, 1871-1971 (pp. 136-179). Chicago: Aldine.

Tversky, A., & Kahneman, D. (1974). Judgment under Uncertainty: Heuristics and Biases. Science, 185(4157), 1124-1131.

United Nations. (2020). World Population Prospects. United Nations Department of Economic and Social Affairs.

Veblen, T. (1899). The Theory of the Leisure Class. Macmillan.

Wilson, D. S. (1975). A Theory of Group Selection. Proceedings of the National Academy of Sciences, 72(1), 143-146.

Credits

Evolutionary Foundations of Wealth

Buss, D. M. (2019). *Evolutionary Psychology: The New Science of the Mind* (5th ed.). Routledge.

The Origins of Wealth

Buss, D. M. (2019). *Evolutionary Psychology: The New Science of the Mind* (5th ed.). Routledge.

Reputation and Social Capital

Tomasello, M. (2009). *Why We Cooperate*. MIT Press.
Buss, D. M. (2019). *Evolutionary Psychology: The New Science of the Mind* (5th ed.). Routledge.

Mating Strategies and Economic Behaviour

Buss, D. M. (1989). Sex Differences in Human Mate Preferences: Evolutionary Hypotheses Tested in 37 Cultures. *Behavioral and Brain Sciences*, 12(1), 1-49.
Hitsch, G. J., Hortaçsu, A., & Ariely, D. (2010). Matching and Sorting in Online Dating. *American Economic Review*, 100(1), 130-163.

Parental Investment and Wealth Transmission

Trivers, R. L. (1972). Parental Investment and Sexual Selection. In B. Campbell (Ed.), *Sexual Selection and the Descent of Man, 1871-1971* (pp. 136-179). Chicago: Aldine.

Sarpong, P. (1974). *Ghana in Retrospect: Some Aspects of Ghanaian Culture*. Accra: Ghana Publishing Corporation.

Social Alliances and Wealth Preservation

Trivers, R. L. (1971). The Evolution of Reciprocal Altruism. *Quarterly Review of Biology*, 46(1), 35-57.

Fehr, E., & Fischbacher, U. (2003). The nature of human altruism. *Nature*, 425(6960), 785-791.

Risk-Taking and Innovation

Kahneman, D., & Tversky, A. (1979). Prospect Theory: An Analysis of Decision under Risk. *Econometrica*, 47(2), 263-291.

Competition and Cooperation

Hamilton, W. D. (1964). The Genetical Evolution of Social Behavior. I & II. *Journal of Theoretical Biology*, 7(1), 1-52.

Wilson, D. S. (1975). A Theory of Group Selection. *Proceedings of the National Academy of Sciences*, 72(1), 143-146.

Psychological Mechanisms of Wealth Perception

Barber, B. M., & Odean, T. (2001). Boys Will Be Boys: Gender, Overconfidence, and Common Stock Investment. *Quarterly Journal of Economics*, 116(1), 261-292.

Kahneman, D., & Tversky, A. (1979). Prospect Theory: An Analysis of Decision under Risk. *Econometrica*, 47(2), 263-291.

Tversky, A., & Kahneman, D. (1974). Judgment under Uncertainty: Heuristics and Biases. *Science*, 185(4157), 1124-1131.

Cultural Evolution and Economic Systems

Hofstede, G. (2001). *Culture's Consequences: Comparing Values, Behaviors, Institutions, and Organizations Across Nations*. Sage Publications.

Inglehart, R., & Baker, W. E. (2000). Modernization, Cultural Change, and the Persistence of Traditional Values. *American Sociological Review*, 65(1), 19-51.

Schwab, K. (2016). *The Fourth Industrial Revolution*. World Economic Forum.

Wealth, Health, and Longevity

Marmot, M. G., & Wilkinson, R. G. (2005). *Social Determinants of Health*. Oxford University Press.

Sapolsky, R. M. (2004). *Why Zebras Don't Get Ulcers: The Acclaimed Guide to Stress, Stress-Related Diseases, and Coping*. Henry Holt and Co.

The Future of Wealth in an Evolutionary Context

Harari, Y. N. (2015). *Sapiens: A Brief History of Humankind*. Harper.

United Nations. (2020). *World Population Prospects*. United Nations Department of Economic and Social Affairs.

Published by Lulu Press, Inc
627 Davis Drive Suite 300
Morrisville, NC 27560
United States

+1 844 212 0689
www.lulu.com

ISBN: 978-0-244-66647-7